THE AUCKLAND BOOK.

Nigel Beckford
Michael Fitzsimons
Concepts, Art Direction, Text

Patrick Fitzsimons
Research, Text

Alisha Brunton
Jess Lunnon
Sandi Mackechnie
Cynthia Merhej
Ivy Niu
Sarah Ryan
Ezra Whittaker-Powley
Illustrations

By George, It's Auckland!

In 1840, Governor William Hobson named
Auckland after his boss, the First Lord of the Admiralty,
the Earl of Auckland, George Eden. Lord Auckland was a
three-time First Lord of the Admiralty and also served as
Governor-General of India between 1836 and 1842.

THE AUCKLAND BOOK

Published 2014 by FitzBeck Publishing
www.theaucklandbook.co.nz

Contact
Tel: 04 8019669
PO Box 10399, The Terrace, Wellington 6143

ISBN: 978-0-473-28603-3

How do you draw Auckland?

You get walking and driving …. everywhere. A bunch of you, heading in all directions, over many months.

You take in the grand circle views from Mangere Mountain, One Tree Hill and North Head. You journey up and down Great South Road like it's your own driveway, you cross-cross the bridge many times, you head for the bush and black sands of the wild West. You visit the beaches, the malls and the markets.

You walk the Wynyard, dine at the Depot, settle in at the Gypsy Tearooms and the Blue Breeze. You get out on the harbour where there are more boats per head of population than anywhere else in the world. You drop in at the cathedrals and roar on the Warriors. You feel the blast of the market where a run-down fixer-upper is about to go for well over the mill. You amble along the Shore's coastal walkway.

You cast your mind back to earlier days, to the movers and shakers of yesteryear. You remember the huge events – the America's Cup and the Rugby World Cup, the big concerts and community celebrations when half the city hit the town.

You witness the daily transformation of landscape and skyline. You feel the pull of a city that is becoming a magnet for people from all over the world.

You ask family and friends, bar staff and baristas, taxi-drivers and real estate agents, musicians and executives, what makes the place tick. What would they draw?

And then you apply a ton of imagination. You put together a team of illustrators and challenge them to capture the Auckland your camera can't. You warn them they are up for a mountain of work. You sketch and refine, you debate colour palettes and perspectives, you swap files and ideas endlessly.

Eventually, you assemble a giant, panoramic vision of a young city on a roll. An aqua-tinted South Pacific metropolis like no other, thriving on a narrow neck of land.

You discover a city that is not just a great place to live but an intriguing place to draw.

And then you cross your fingers and hope people like it.

Arohanui

Michael Fitzsimons   Nigel Beckford

(aka FitzBeck)

Ngāti Pāoa

Ngāti Whātua-o-Ōrākei

Ngāi Tai

Te Kawerau-a-Maki

Te Wai-o-Hua

Ngāti Te Ata

ISTHMUS OF A THOUSAND LOVERS

The Tamaki isthmus was settled by Māori around 1350. Open to the sea on both sides, with very fertile soil & 49 ready-made volcanic forts, it was a strategic place to hold & hotly contested. Hence its popular Māori name: Tāmaki Makau Rau, the isthmus of a thousand lovers.

By the 17th century the Tamaki iwi had terraced the cones, built pa, and developed 2,000 hectares of kumara gardens. Today it is home to 6 iwi: Ngāti Pāoa, Ngāi Tai, Te Wai-o-Hua, Ngāti Whātua-o-Ōrākei, Ngāti Te Ata & Te Kawerau-a-Maki.

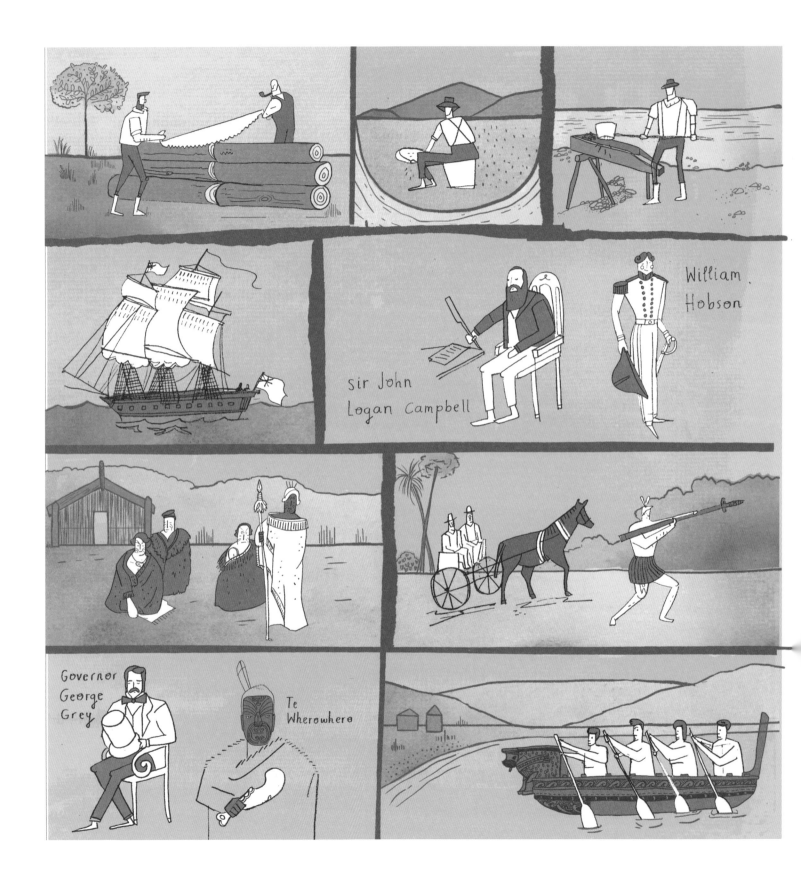

COLO-NIAL DAYS

The arrival of Europeans, with disease and muskets, dramatically changed inter-tribal relations on the Tamaki isthmus. In 1750, with 20,000 residents, it was New Zealand's most wealthy and prosperous area. By 1840 it had become a depopulated buffer zone, with a population less than 500. Auckland enjoyed an uneasy tenure as New Zealand's second capital. It was physically isolated and considered a financial drain on the rest of the colony. By the time prosperity came to the city, with booming timber, gum, and gold exports, the capital had shifted to Wellington.

AMBER CITY

Before human arrival, 1.6 million hectares of Kauri forests covered the top half of the north island; now, thanks to 800 years of slash-and-burn and 200 of logging, only 7,000 hectares remain, with very few in Auckland. By the end of the 19th century sawmilling was the largest source of employment in the region, with Auckland supplying 91.5% of NZ's timber exports. In truth, though, Auckland City was built on Kauri gum, aka NZ amber: 450,000 tons were exported from the city between 1850-1900, its largest export.

EARLY MĀORI FAVOURED SETTLING ON AUCKLAND'S VOLCANIC CONES BECAUSE OF THE FERTILE SOIL CREATED BY THE HISTORIC LAVA FLOWS, AS WELL AS FOR DEFENCE PURPOSES AND GOOD VIEWS. ONE OF THE BEST PRESERVED OF THESE CONES, AND BEST TO VISIT, IS MANGERE MOUNTAIN. ONCE THE SITE OF THE LARGEST POLYNESIAN SETTLEMENT IN THE SOUTH PACIFIC, THE REMAINS OF AN EXTENSIVE PA, WITH ITS TERRACES AND BORDER GARDENS, CAN STILL BE SEEN TODAY, AS WELL AS THE COW-PAT SHAPED 'LAVA BOMBS' THAT LANDED HERE DURING THE MOUNTAIN'S CONCEPTION.

MANGERE MOUNTAIN

Known to PEERS as THE 'FATHER OF AUCKLAND' SIR Logan Campbell ARRIVED IN 1840, BUILT the CITY'S FIRST house, ACACIA Cottage, AND opened THE first SHOP. HE WAS everything AUCKLAND LIKES in A man — a BUSINESS EXPERT, a globetrotter, physically VIGOROUS (ON HIS 60TH BIRTHDAY HE VAULTED HIS FARM'S FIVE- BARRED GATE) and a REAL estate visionary. IN 1853 he bought a 1000 ACRE SUBURBAN FARM and CALLED IT One Tree Hill. LATE IN LIFE, HE MADE PART OF THIS LAND HIS CORNWALL Park LEGACY, and WAS born.

John Logan Campbell

BOOMING

Auckland contributes $70 billion – 36% of GDP – to the NZ economy!

BALMY

Auckland is the warmest of the main centres with over 2,000 hours of sunshine a year. The average maximum temperature is 23.7°C in summer and 14.5°C in winter.

WELCOME TO AUCKLAND

POPULAR

Auckland consistently ranks in the top ten of the world's major cities in terms of quality of life. 70% of newcomers to the country settle in Auckland.

GOOD FOR THE GARDEN

Auckland's 137 days of rain annually (1,240mm) create ideal growing conditions. The local Botanic Garden sustains over 10,000 plants from around the world.

HEADING OUTDOORS

Aucklanders enjoy the natural grandeur of 26 regional parks covering a massive 40,000 hectares. Closer to home there are over 4,000 local parks and sports parks.

TRACK 1
2.5 HOURS

TRACK 2
1 HOUR

ON A ROLL

Between 2006 to 2013 Auckland's population increased by 10% and house values rose nearly 20%. The Super City is planning to house an additional 1 million people over the next 30 years. By 2031, 38 in every 100 Kiwis will be Aucklanders.

AFLOAT

OVER 60,000 OF THE NATION'S 150,000 REGISTERED YACHTIES ARE AUCKLANDERS. AUCKLAND IS A 'WATER CITY', BOASTING NEARLY 4,000KMS OF COASTLINE, 2 HARBOURS, A GULF, A SEA & 21,000KMS OF RIVERS & STREAMS.

CITY SLICK-ERS

90% OF AUCKLANDERS LIVE IN URBAN AREAS, ALTHOUGH 80% OF THE REGION'S TOTAL LAND MASS IS RURAL & GREEN FIELDS.

A MAGNET

34% (1.5 MILLION) OF NEW ZEALAND'S POPULATION LIVE IN THE QUEEN CITY. THE REGION'S POPULATION IS EXPECTED TO GROW BY A THIRD BY 2031.

DIVERSE
ASIAN
POLYNESIAN

POLYNESIAN

Auckland has the largest Polynesian population in the world. 179,000 Pacific people live in Auckland (14% of the population). In 30 years time, it is estimated 1 in 5 Aucklanders will be of Pacific descent.

DIVERSE

40% of Aucklanders were born overseas. Auckland is home to 150 ethnic identities and 120 languages.

ASIAN

Auckland has the highest Asian population in the country. 23% by 2021. 27 out of every 100 Aucklanders will be of Asian descent.

WITHIN A 20 KILOMETRE RADIUS OF the CITY, there are 49 discrete VOLCANIC CONES, all evidence of the AUCKLAND VOLCANIC FIELD (AVF) UNDERNEATH. SOME OF THESE are WELL-PRESERVED. BUT OTHERS HAVE BEEN ALMOST entirely LEVELLED DUE to QUARRYING.

EARLY settlers built Walls with VOLCANIC SCORIA, & IN THE LATE 19th CENTURY VOLCANIC BASALT WAS USED TO CONSTRUCT the MT EDEN PRISON (CURRENTLY DORMANT, IT REMAINED ACTIVE UNTIL 2011).

Today about 20% OF THE AGGREGATE FOR NZ ROADS IS QUARRIED FROM AUCKLAND's VOLCANOES. BECAUSE IT's A MONOGENETIC field, NONE OF THESE VOLCANOES are likely to blow again. STILL YOUNG and ACTIVE, though, IT REMAINS possible THAT MAGMA FROM THE AVF WILL RISE to the SURFACE & POP UP A NEW RANGITOTO.

Rangitoto

North Head

Mount Eden

One Tree Hill

CITY OF VOLCANOES.

Mangere Mountain

HOBSON ST GREAT SOUTH RD

QUEEN ST

ONEWA RD

REMUE

EAST COAST RD

GREAT NORTH R

QUAY ST

KARANGAHAPE

RA RD

TAMAKI DR

KHYBER PASS

DOMINION RD

ORAKEI RD PONSONBY RD

AUCKLANDERS DREAMT OF BRIDGING THE HARBOUR SINCE THEY FIRST ARRIVED. THE NORTH SHORE LOOKED PROMISING. IN 1860 A PROPOSAL FOR A FLOATING DESIGN WAS REJECTED OVER COST CONCERNS. A HUNDRED YEARS LATER SIMILAR CONCERNS WOULD RESTRICT THE ULTIMATE DESIGN TO FOUR LANES AND NO FOOTPATHS — WITHIN SIX YEARS TRAFFIC WAS THREE TIMES MORE THAN EXPECTED. JAPANESE INGENUITY BROUGHT THE 'NIPPON CLIP-ONS' IN 1969: TWO EXTRA LANES ATTACHED TO EACH SIDE, DOUBLING CAPACITY. TODAY TRAFFIC CONGESTION IS AGAIN SEVERE, (170,000 CARS CROSS PER DAY), THOUGH ALMOST 40% OF PEOPLE CROSSING BETWEEN 7 AND 9 A.M ARE NOW SITTING IN BUSES. THIS HAS ENCOURAGED THE CITY TO CONSIDER AN UNDERWATER TUNNEL.

Anniversary

Auckland EARNS ITS CITY OF Sails MONIKER WITH THIS ANNUAL SHOWCASE OF ITS STANDING ARMADA:

REGATTA

ALL SHIPS BOATS, DINGHIES, Catamarans, SLOOPS, DRAGON BOATS AND WAKA.

FIRST HELD IN 1840, THE EVENT HAS BECOME THE LARGEST SINGLE DAY REGATTA IN THE WORLD.

Queen Street

AUCKLAND'S MOST FAMOUS STREET (NAMED AFTER QUEEN VICTORIA) IN THE HEART OF THE CBD, STARTS AT QUEEN'S WHARF AND RUNS FOR 3 KILOMETRES (A 'GOLDEN MILE') UPHILL TO KARANGAHAPE ROAD. THE MOST EXPENSIVE REAL ESTATE ON THE NZ MONOPOLY BOARD, QUEEN STREET REMAINS AUCKLAND'S MOST PEDESTRIAN-FILLED STREET. AN ESTIMATED 40,000 PEOPLE WALK UP AND DOWN IT EVERYDAY.

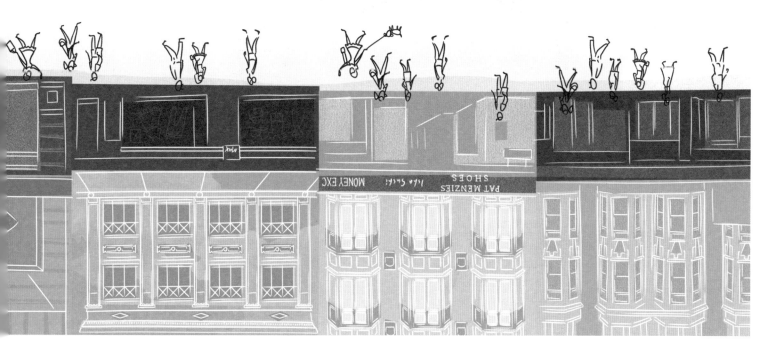

K'ROAD

PRIOR TO THE MOTORWAY BOOM OF THE 50s, K'ROAD WAS AUCKLAND'S PREMIER SHOPPING STRIP.

HEN EXPANDING SUBURBIA AND THE INNER-CITY MOTORWAY FORCED 50,000
OCALS OUT, K'ROAD TRANSFORMED INTO THE CITY'S SEEDIEST RED-LIGHT
ISTRICT. WAVES OF GENTRIFICATION IN RECENT DECADES HAVE MADE THE
RIP MORE PALATABLE AGAIN, BUT IT REMAINS A FAVOURITE SPOT FOR
AUCKLAND'S ALTERNATIVES, TRANSGENDERED, FRINGE ARTISTS,
LGBTs, OP SHOPPERS, AND ECCENTRICS.
NE TRANSLATION OF THE MĀORI NAME IS SIMPLY "THE WINDING
RIDGE OF HUMAN ACTIVITY."

THOUGH CARVED AWAY OVER TIME BY THE MOTORWAY, GRAFTON REMAINS HOME TO SOME OF AUCKLAND'S MOST HISTORIC SITES - THE OLDEST BOWLING GREENS IN THE SOUTHERN HEMISPHERE, THE OLDEST UNIVERSITY IN THE NORTH ISLAND, THE CITY'S ORIGINAL CEMETERY, FIRST HOSPITAL AND PARK.

BUILT IN 1910, THE GRAFTON BRIDGE WAS ONCE THE LARGEST REINFORCED-CONCRETE ARCHED STRUCTURE IN THE WORLD.

HISTORIC GRAFTON

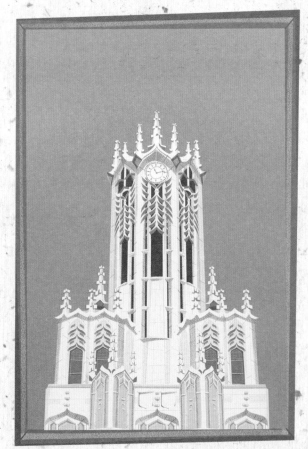

APARTMENT LIVING

AUCKLAND'S CBD APARTMENT DWELLERS ARE A GROWING PHENOMENON: AT LAST COUNT THEY HAD QUADRUPLED, WITH 100,000 APARTMENTS NOW MAKING UP AROUND A QUARTER OF AUCKLAND'S DWELLINGS.

THEY ARE STUDENTS AND PROFESSIONALS, AUCKLAND'S MODERN TRANSIENTS: 95%
HAVE A QUALIFICATION; 50% ARE UNDER 30; 50% ARE ASIAN; 44% WALK OR JOG TO
WORK; AND 93% LIVED SOMEWHERE ELSE 5 YEARS AGO. THE QUALITY OF APARTMENTS
RANGE FROM 'SHOEBOX-SIZED' 25 SQ M UNITS WITHOUT BALCONIES TO VIADUCT
BASIN PENTHOUSES WORTH MILLIONS.

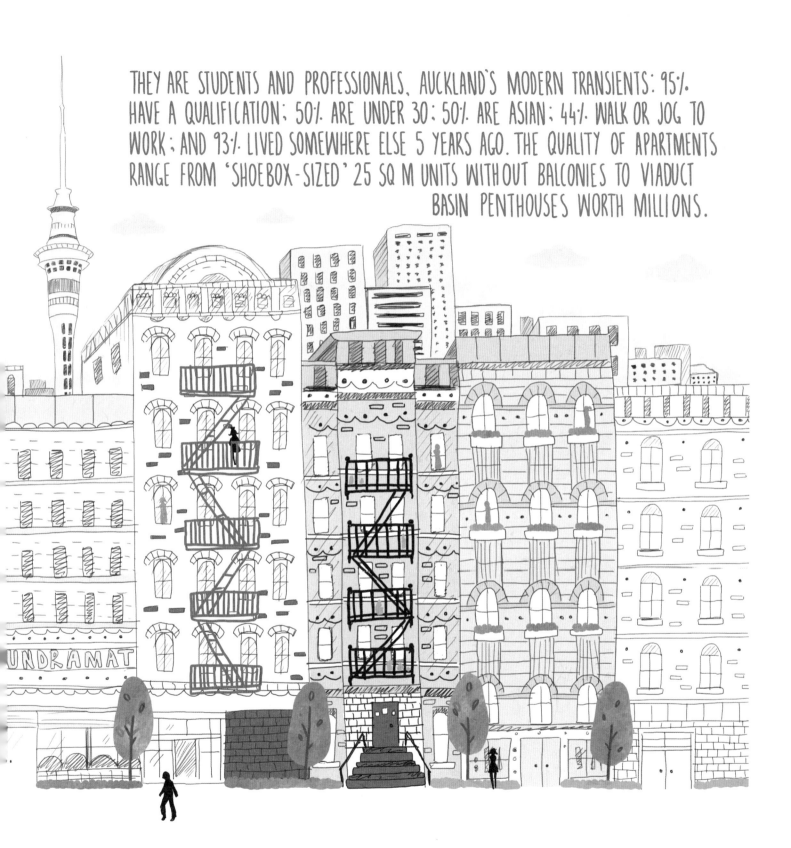

SKYTOWER

AT 328 METRES, SKY TOWER IS THE TALLEST MAN-MADE, FREE-STANDING STRUCTURE IN THE SOUTHERN HEMISPHERE, OFFERING BREATHTAKING VIEWS FOR UP TO 80KMS IN ALL DIRECTIONS.

THE ADVENTUROUS CAN SKYWALK AROUND THE PERGOLA AT 192 METRES UP OR SKY-JUMP OFF THE TOWER. SKYTOWER IS ILLUMINATED AT NIGHT IN STRIKING COLOURS TO MARK EVENTS SUCH AS CHRISTMAS, ST PATRICK'S DAY AND CHINESE NEW YEAR.

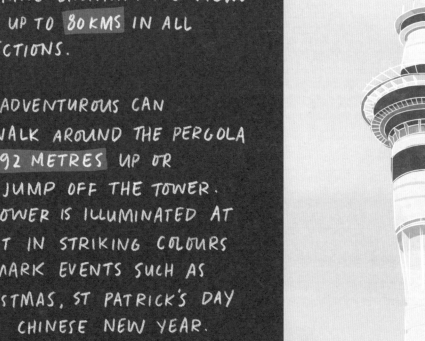

AUCKLAND

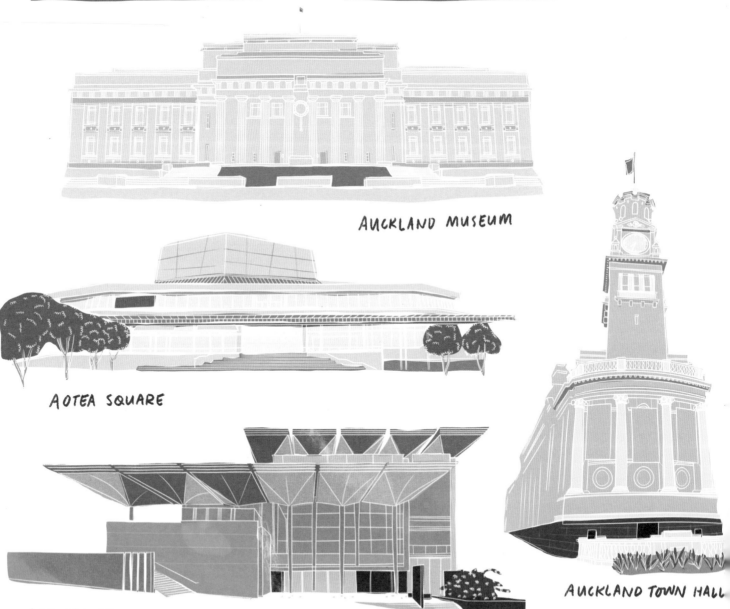

AUCKLAND MUSEUM

AOTEA SQUARE

ART GALLERY

AUCKLAND TOWN HALL

LANDMARKS

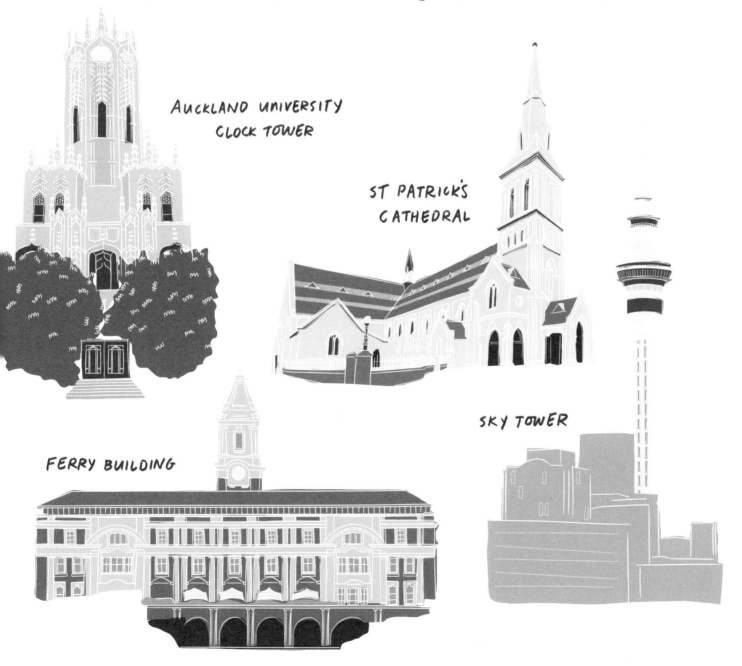

AUCKLAND UNIVERSITY CLOCK TOWER

ST PATRICK'S CATHEDRAL

SKY TOWER

FERRY BUILDING

Wynyard Quarter

Auckland's waterfront is undergoing massive rejuvenation. Tank Farm, once one of the most industrial parts of the Western Reclamation, has become Wynyard Quarter, a 37-hectare public space complete with 'industrial chic' sculpture, walkways, playgrounds and even waterfront tai chi and yoga classes. The petro-chemical storage facilities are now Silo Park, a trendy music venue, vibrant night market and outdoor cinema. Nearby, the thriving Auckland Fish Market sells the catch of the day.

The Viaduct Basin has undergone a meteoric transformation in recent times. Once home to shipyards, abattoirs, and lime traders, this neglected area at the foot of Freeman's Bay benefited greatly from Black Magic's America's Cup triumph in 1995. The Viaduct Basin was

created to accommodate the next challenge in 2000. Overnight, upmarket restaurants, bars and apartments sprung up around the marina of luxury yachts and super-yachts. The Viaduct Basin is now a favourite destination for party-goers, tourists and locals alike.

RANGITOTO

The largest & youngest of Auckland's 50-plus volcanoes, Rangitoto's symmetrical cone has been an iconic landmark since it was born 600 years ago. In 2 eruptions, each lasting several years, Rangitoto rose from the sea beside the much older Motutapu Island. Today, Rangitoto Science Reserve is pest-free & home to New Zealand's largest pohutakawa forest.

Rangitoto isn't expected to blow again, though the Auckland volcanic field as a whole remains young & active.

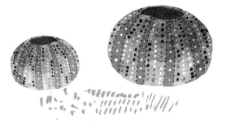

Kelly Tarlton's

KELLY TARLTON WAS AN ADVENTURER, SELF-TAUGHT
DIVER, AND TREASURE HUNTER WHO SOMEHOW SET UP
ONE OF THE WORLD'S MOST INNOVATIVE AQUARIUMS IN
DISUSED SEWAGE TANKS BENEATH TAMAKI DRIVE. LIKE
FRENCH OCEANOGRAPHER JACQUES COUSTEAU, IT WAS
KELLY'S DREAM TO GIVE THE PUBLIC A TASTE OF WHAT
HE EXPERIENCED BENEATH THE WATER. KELLY TARLTON'S
UNDERWATER WORLD, WHICH OPENED IN 1985, PIONEERED
THE USE OF CURVED ACRYLIC TUNNELS, WHICH ALLOWED
PEOPLE TO OBSERVE THE FISH FROM BELOW.
STILL HUMMING, THE AQUARIUM HAS NOW HOSTED
12 MILLION VISITORS. IT'S THE PLACE KIWI KIDS ARE
MOST LIKELY TO MEET A KING PENGUIN.

Harbour views, peace and quiet and proximity to central Auckland have turned Herne Bay and Saint Mary's Bay into some of Auckland's most sought-after and expensive real estate. Herne Bay was NZ's first suburb with a $2 million house. In recent years, the tastefully-renovated historic villas have been joined by new mutli-level mansions. When Bishop Pompallier bought 19 hectares of the area in 1853, all he could hear were the birds in the pohutakawas. By 1959, a 10-lane motorway at the foot of the bay led to the Harbour Bridge.

A Decent Send-off

YOU KNOW YOU'VE REALLY MADE IT IN NEW ZEALAND WHEN YOUR FUNERAL IS HELD AT HOLY TRINITY CATHEDRAL, PARNELL. NEW ZEALAND BIDS FAREWELL TO ITS MOST ILLUSTRIOUS SONS, SUCH AS SIR EDMUND HILLARY AND SIR PAUL HOLMES, FROM THE MAGNIFICENT ANGLICAN CATHEDRAL WHICH SITS ATOP THE PARNELL RISE.

HOLY TRINITY IS DESCRIBED AS THE WORLD'S ONLY EXAMPLE OF 'PACIFIC GOTHIC' ARCHITECTURE.

Grammar Zone Fever

AUCKLAND'S SCHOOL SYSTEM IS STRATIFIED AND HIGHLY COMPETITIVE. SOME SCHOOLS HAVE BECOME SO DESIRABLE THEIR ZONE CATCHMENTS DISTORT REAL ESTATE PRICES. AGENTS REPORT PARENTS PAYING 'PREMIUMS' OF BETWEEN $150,000 TO $300,000 FOR PROPERTY THAT SITS INSIDE THE AUCKLAND GRAMMAR AND EPSOM GIRLS' GRAMMAR CATCHMENTS. PRESSURE FOR PLACES IS SUCH THAT SOME PARENTS EVEN FALSIFY DOCUMENTS AND GIVE FAKE ADDRESSES TO ENROL CHILDREN. AUCKLAND GRAMMAR HAS A FULL-TIME PRIVATE INVESTIGATOR WORKING ON SUCH CASES. THE BALLOT FOR 'OUT OF ZONE' PLACES IS HELD UNDER POLICE SUPERVISION.

BRITOMART

TEN YEARS AFTER OPENING TO THE PUBLIC, THE MUCH DEBATED BRITOMART TRANSPORT HUB IS A SUCCESS AND A FOCAL POINT FOR REJUVENATION IN THE CENTRAL CITY.

A NEW 6.5 HECTARE WATERFRONT SHOPPING PRECINCT OF TRENDY EATERIES, BARS, FASHION AND BEAUTY BOUTIQUES AND SPECIALTY STORES IS ALSO FLOURISHING NEARBY.

THE AREA TAKES ITS NAME FROM THE EXTINCT POINT BRITOMART (LEVELLED FOR THE RAILWAY), NAMED BY MĀORI TE RERENGA ORA ITI, THE LEAP OF THE FEW SURVIVORS.

ST. KEVINS ARCADE

1924

THE NEO-GREEK STYLE SHOPPING ARCADE, DESIGNED IN THE 1920s, IS NOW A SHRINE TO ALL THINGS 'INDIE' - A BOHEMIAN PRECINCT OF VINTAGE CLOTHING, SECOND HAND BOOKS, FASHION, FOOD AND MUSIC. DOWNSTAIRS MUSIC VENUES THE WINE CELLAR/WHAMMY BAR COMPLETE THE ALTERNATIVE EXPERIENCE IN SUITABLE DINGY STYLE.
STEPS AT THE REAR OF THE BUILDING PROVIDE A THOROUGHFARE FROM K'ROAD TO THE GRASSY SLOPES OF MYERS PARK.

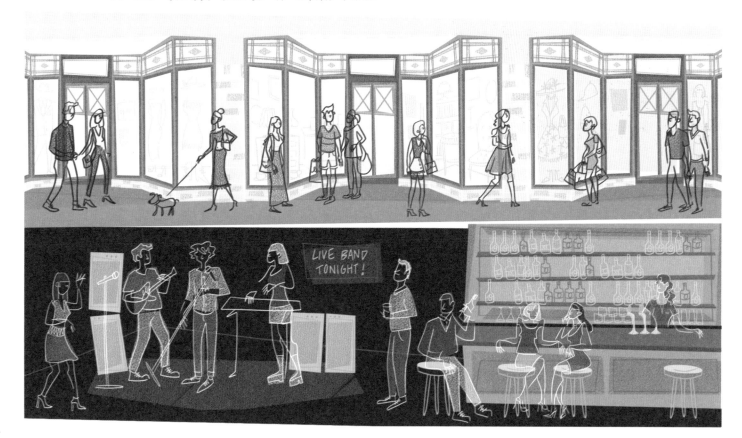

ESPLANADE HOTEL

THE BUNKER

NORTH HEAD LANDMARK

Restaurants

Coffee & Chocolates

MAIN STREET

HOUSES & VILLAS

NAVY SHIP

P3569

FERRY & WHARF

DEVONPORT

THOUGH SETTLED SINCE 1836, DEVONPORT, THE NORTH SHORE'S FIRST SUBURB, EVOLVED IN ISOLATION. AUCKLANDERS USED TO CALL IT 'THE ISLAND'; RESIDENTS WERE FERRY PEOPLE; THE RNZ NAVY MADE IT HOME.

IT WASN'T UNTIL THE COMPLETION OF THE HARBOUR BRIDGE IN 1959 THAT DEVONPORT STARTED TO LOOK LIKE THE REST OF THE CITY, WITH FERRY NUMBERS PLUMMETING AND RAPID GROWTH. STILL, IT HAS RETAINED A LOT OF PRE-BRIDGE CHARM, AND NEW FERRIES NOW TAKE A LOT OF MAINLANDERS THERE TO SHOP, DINE AND DRINK BY THE WATER. HOME OF THE LEGENDARY DEVONPORT FOLK CLUB, WHICH HAS HOSTED CONCERTS IN ITS 1891 'RUSSIAN INVASION SCARE' ERA BUNKER FOR OVER 40 YEARS.

BROWNS BAY CARSON BAY

TORBAY WAIAKE

〜 ROTHESAY BAY 〜

MAIRANGI BAY

CAMPBELLS MILFORD BEACH
BAY TAKAPUNA MURRAYS
BEACH BAY

THE SHORE

BEFORE THE HARBOUR BRIDGE ARRIVED IN 1959 ONLY 50,000 PEOPLE LIVED ON THE NORTH SHORE. IT BOOMED THEREAFTER AND WAS NZ'S FOURTH LARGEST CITY (225,000) PRIOR TO AMALGAMATION. THE AREA'S BAYS AND BEACHES ARE A GLOBAL MAGNET - 40% OF RESIDENTS WERE BORN OVERSEAS, 10% ARE SOUTH AFRICAN AND KOREAN IS THE SECOND MOST SPOKEN LANGUAGE. THE 23KMS NORTH SHORE COASTAL WALK TAKES YOU ALL THE WAY, TIDES PERMITTING, FROM LONG BAY TO DEVONPORT.

Wintergardens

THE STYLISH WINTERGARDENS COMPLEX IS SITUATED IN THE CITY'S OLDEST PARK, THE AUCKLAND DOMAIN. BUILT AFTER WORLD WAR I, THE COMPLEX FEATURES TWO LARGE GLASSHOUSES - FOR TEMPERATE AND TROPICAL PLANTS. IN BETWEEN IS AN ELEGANT COURTYARD WITH CLASSICAL STATUES AND A SUNKEN POND.

Remmers

One of New Zealand's most exclusive neighbourhoods, a home in Remuera has been highly desirable since the early 14th century. Apart from a brief window in the 1840s, however, real estate has always been tough to get your hands on - last year a modest two-bedroom brick-and-tile unit went for over $900k. Though its highly fertile soil might be a little under-utilised today, it's the best place in the country to spot a Remuera tractor (SUV.) After a century of gentrification, 'Remmers' is renowned these days for its leafy mansions and an array of exclusive medical specialists.

the domain

THE DOMAIN IS THE CITY'S OLDEST PARK, AND AT 75 HECTARES ONE OF ITS LARGEST. ITS MOST DISTINCTIVE FEATURES TODAY ARE THE AUCKLAND WAR MUSEUM AND THE CENOTAPH, AS WELL AS THE POPULAR WINTERGARDENS. OVER THE YEARS THE DOMAIN HAS HOSTED SOME OF AUCKLAND'S LARGEST EVENTS, FROM ROYAL AND PAPAL VISITS, TO NIGHT TIME SYMPHONIES AND CHRISTMAS CAROLS FOR CROWDS OF UP TO 200,000.

mission bay

A 15-minute drive to the east of the city along Tamaki Drive brings you to Mission Bay. All year round, this vibrant beachfront is a favourite for walkers, windsurfers, sailors and swimmers. Mission Bay features a grand art deco fountain and a spectacular view of the perfectly symmetrical Rangitoto island. The Melanesian Mission House at the bay was built in 1858 from Rangitoto's volcanic stone.

AUCKLAND
CENTRAL

ROUND THE BAYS RUN

HOBSON BAY

OKAHU BAY

MISSION BAY

ORAKEI BASIN

NZ's LARGEST MASS PARTICIPATION SPORTING EVENT (70,000 STRONG) IS NOW OVER 40 YEARS OLD.

ONCE A YEAR ABOUT 70,000 ATHLETES RUN OR WALK 8.4KM AROUND WAITEMATA HARBOUR, WITH ALL PROCEEDS GOING TO A CHILDREN'S CHARITY.

SOME TEAMS LESS INTERESTED IN PBs CHOOSE TO RUN IN COSTUME.

AFTER THE RACE, 600 BARBECUES FEED THE FINISHERS.

ST.HELIER'S BAY

THE MAN IN RED

Every year, 50,000 Aucklanders cram the CBD for the Farmers Santa Parade, which began in 1934, a gift to the city's children from Farmers' founder Robert Laidlaw. For 2.2 kilometres floats of every description, pipe bands, fairies, clowns, celebrities and inflatable superheroes entertain the masses until Santa's triumphant arrival on his sled.

Takaparawhau in Māori, Bastion Point overlooks all Waitemata Harbour's incoming traffic. Originally occupied by Ngāti Whātua, the land was taken piece-by-piece by the Crown from the 1850s for defence purposes. In 1976, however, no longer worried about invasion, the Crown proposed the development of high-income housing on the Point. This instigated a 506-day protest by Joe Hawke's Orakei Maori Action Committee. The non-violent occupation, and ultimate eviction, is considered a watershed in the Māori protest movement for land rights. Nearly ten years later the Waitangi Tribunal, in deciding its first historical claim, returned most of Takaparawhau to Ngāti Whātua, with a formal apology.

KEEP
→
RIGHT

EVEN BEFORE WWII, AUCKLAND BOASTED ONE OF THE HIGHEST CAR-OWNERSHIP RATES IN THE WORLD AND THE LOVE AFFAIR WITH CARS HAS NEVER CEASED. 900,000-PLUS CARS USE AUCKLAND'S EXTENSIVE MOTORWAY NETWORK EVERY DAY AND MORE THAN 90% OF JOURNEYS ARE UNDERTAK BY CARS. MAJOR INVESTMENT IN ROADING AND PUBLIC TRANSPORT IS UNDER WAY TO DEAL WITH THE CITY'S LEGENDARY TRAFFIC CONGESTION, AND THERE'S PLENTY MORE TO COME. MASSIVE TRANSPORT PROJECTS, WITH A PRICE TAG OF AROUND $10 BILLION, ARE BEING PUSHED BY GOVERNMENT TO SPEED UP TRAFFIC FLOWS ON MAJOR HIGHWAYS, EASE FREIGHT ACCESS TO THE AIRPORT AND PROVIDE A SECOND WAITEMATA HARBOUR CROSSING.

motoring on

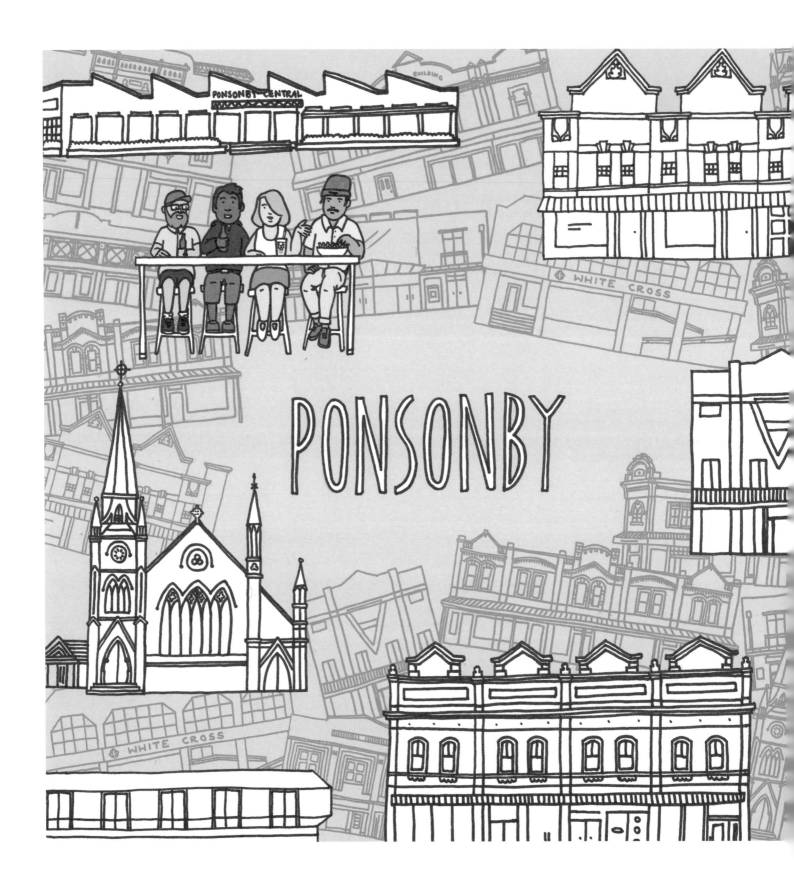

WHITE CROSS

ORIGINALLY CALLED DEDWOOD, PONSONBY WAS ONE OF AUCKLAND'S FIRST SUBURBS. AFTER THE STOCK MARKET CRASH OF 1893, IT WAS DESERTED AND BECAME A SLUM IN THE FIRST HALF OF THE 20TH CENTURY. URBAN RENEWAL SCHEMES OF THE '50S REPLACED COTTAGES WITH CHEAP FLATS AND TOWNHOUSES AND IN THE 1970s THERE WAS AN INFLUX OF POLYNESIAN FAMILIES, ARTISTS AND BOHEMIANS, ATTRACTED BY THE LOW RENTS. ALTHOUGH MOST OF THIS POPULATION MOVED ON WITH GENTRIFICATION IN THE '80s, THE SUBURB STILL RETAINS A REPUTATION FOR 'COLOUR'. VISITING TODAY YOU'RE MOST LIKELY TO NOTICE THE TRENDY CAFÉS, RESTAURANTS, AND BARS OF THE SELF-PROCLAIMED 'HIPPEST' SUBURB IN AUCKLAND.

PONSONBY BUILDING 1911

Aucklanders have been fascinated by horses ever since Samuel Marsden unloaded them in Tamaki in 1814. The first race meeting at Ellerslie was held in 1874, and race days have featured prominently on the Auckland social calendar ever since. Every year thousands of Aucklanders flock to Auckland Cup Week to enjoy the city's biggest and most fashionable party, as well as the thrill of live racing.

Race Fashions

EDEN PARK
All Black Fortress

Originally Cabbage Patch Tree Swamp, Eden Park was brought to life by some visionary drainage by the Kingsland Cricket Club in 1900. Within a few years, rugby was introduced and today's renovated stadium is the home of NZ rugby. As the largest stadium in the country, it takes the lion's share of important sporting events-

the final rugby test of every tour; the 1992 & 2015 Cricket World Cup semis and the 1987 & 2011 Rugby World Cup triumphs. The All Blacks' winning record at the park (unbeaten since 1994) has earned the stadium 'fortress' status.

CORNWALL CRICKET CLUB IS ONE OF NEW ZEALAND'S OLDEST AND MOST FAMOUS CRICKET GROUNDS, SITUATED IN IDYLLIC CORNWALL PARK. THE CHARMING SETTING AND PAVILLION REMIND MANY OF ENGLAND, BUT WITH BETTER WEATHER. ORIGINALLY AN EPSOM PIONEER HOUSE, THE PAVILLION HAS BEEN THE SCENE OF MANY LEGENDARY AFTER-MATCH FESTIVITIES. CORNWALL PARK HOSTED THE FIRST-EVER GAME OF CRICKET MAX, A FIREWORKS VERSION OF THE GAME DEVISED BY CORNWALL SON, MARTIN CROWE.

ONE TREE HILL

WHEN EUROPEANS ARRIVED, MAUNGAKIEKIE WAS CROWNED BY A SINGLE SACRED TOTARA. IN 1850 IT WAS CHOPPED DOWN BY A SETTLER, PROBABLY FOR BUILDING MATERIAL. CITY FOUNDER JOHN LOGAN CAMPBELL ATTEMPTED TO REPLANT NATIVES ON THE SUMMIT, BUT ONLY TWO PINES, MEANT TO SHELTER THE PURIRI, SURVIVED. LOGAN CAMPBELL ALSO FUNDED AN OBELISK AS A MEMORIAL TO MĀORI WHICH STANDS ON THE SUMMIT OF THE VOLCANO. THE SOLE REMAINING PINE TREE WAS SUBJECT TO SEVERAL CHAINSAW ATTACKS IN THE 1990s. THE SUMMIT IS VERY POPULAR WITH TOURISTS AS IT OFFERS GREAT VIEWS OF BOTH OF AUCKLAND'S HARBOURS.

THE DOG WALKERS OF
MEOLA REEF

Out amongst the mangroves, marshes and mudflats, off Pt Chevalier / Westmere, lies the long-cooled lava of Meola Reef. It was created over 20,000 years ago by volcanic eruptions flowing into the Waitemata harbour. The 15-hectare Reef Reserve includes a hugely popular 'off-leash' exercise park for dogs.

PACIFIC
CHURCH-GOING

THE FIRST PACIFIC CHURCH IN THE COUNTRY WAS THE NEWTON PACIFIC ISLANDERS CONGREGATIONAL CHURCH (PICC) IN EDINBURGH STREET, OFF K'ROAD. IT WAS FOUNDED IN 1947 FOR AUCKLAND'S FIRST 3000 PIs. THE FIRST PACIFIC PEOPLE TO COME TO AUCKLAND SETTLED IN INNER-CITY SUBURBS WHERE THERE WERE JOBS AND CHEAP HOUSING. THE PICC'S CHURCHES, WHICH PROLIFERATED WITH EACH WAVE OF ARRIVALS, BECAME PACIFIC VILLAGES SCATTERED ACROSS THE CITY.

MOTAT, THE MUSEUM OF TRANSPORT & TECHNOLOGY, HAS BEEN GOING **STRONG** SINCE 1964 THANKS TO EFFORTS OF LOCAL VOLUNTEERS. THE MUSEUM'S **LOVINGLY**- RESTORED VINTAGE TRAMS, TRUCKS, TRAINS, PLANES, MOTORBIKES, CARS AND BUSES (MANY <u>IN WORKING ORDER</u>) ARE A **BIG** DRAWCARD FOR VISITORS. MOTAT 2, A RECENT EXTENSION, HOUSES ONE OF THE SOUTHERN HEMISPHERE'S **LARGEST** COLLECTIONS OF VINTAGE AIRCRAFT.

TODAY'S AUCKLAND ZOO WAS BORN IN 1922 WITH THE PURCHASE OF EXOTIC ANIMALS (LIONS, HYENAS, VULTURES, AND MORE) FROM A PRIVATE MENAGERIE IN ONEHUNGA, RUN BY THEN MAYOR JOHN BOYD, THAT WAS THREATENING TO GET OUT OF CONTROL - THE LIONS WERE KNOWN TO BE FED PUKEKO, WEKA, AND CULLED DAIRY COWS. NINETY YEARS LATER THE ZOO'S REPUTATION FOR ANIMAL HUSBANDRY AND CONSERVATION ARE BEYOND REPROACH, AS EXHIBITED IN THE TV SERIES THE ZOO. A RECENT $16 MILLION MAKE-OVER CREATED THE 3.2 HECTARES TE WAO NUI (THE LIVING REALM) ENCLOSURE, A CELEBRATION OF LOCAL NATURE FROM COAST TO HIGH COUNTRY. SINCE 1923, OVER 28 MILLION PEOPLE HAVE VISITED THE ZOO. WHEN ITS SECOND ELEPHANT, KASHIN, DIED IN 2009, 18,000 AUCKLANDERS ATTENDED IN REMEMBRANCE, THE ZOO'S LARGEST EVER SINGLE-DAY ATTENDANCE.

AUCKLAND ZOO

little and friday.

Charming cafe famous for it's superior home-made baking and cabinet food. The doughnuts are a must for anyone with a sweet tooth. Kim Evan's part-time (initially only open on Fridays) venture has blossomed into two cafes in Belmont and Newmarket open seven days a week.
The Newmarket store, eccentrically housed in Martha's Fabrics, offers communal dining at white timber tables, topped with yellow plastic animal figurines and bottles of cinammon-flavoured water. The authors recommend the doughnuts.

LEMON COCONUT CAKE 6.5

STICKYDATE PUDDING 6.5

AFW
street
style

PONSONBY
STREET

PARNELL
STREET

KATE SYLVESTER   HUFFER   SALASAI

KAREN WALKER   TRELISE COOPER   MAAIKE

ZAMBESI

AUCKLAND FASHION WEEK

PART PUBLICITY, PART PERFORMANCE, PART PARTY, NEW ZEALAND FASHION WEEK IS THE NZ FASHION DESIGNER'S ANNUAL OPPORTUNITY TO IMPRESS. THE RUNWAY SHOWS ATTRACT OVER 60 DESIGNERS AND 30,000 PEOPLE EVERY YEAR. NZ FASHION LONG WEEKEND GIVES FASHIONISTAS A CHANCE TO GET THE DROP ON WHAT'S COMING OUT NEXT SEASON. IF YOU WANT TO BE A MODEL, HEADING TO AUCKLAND FOR THE MASS CASTING CALL PRE-FASHION WEEK IS YOUR CHANCE TO MAKE IT BIG.

Party
TOWN

Libertine

La Zeppa

Ponsonby Social Cl[
The Blue Breeze In
The Golden Dawn

Gypsy Tearoom

From upmarket precincts and re-purposed heritage buildings to well-hidden hipster haunts, from the CBD to the 'burbs, Auckland's 'watering holes' cater for every taste, thirst and trend.

Britomart Country Club

De Bretts

As Auckland poet C.K. Stead notes in his poem *Auckland*, it's a city for the 'connoisseur of clouds'. Auckland's coastal climate is the perfect blend of the subtropical and the temperate, with the city enjoying warm, humid summers and mild, damp winters. Auckland is one of New Zealand's sunniest cities but rain-bearing clouds frequently roll in from the surrounding Pacific Ocean. It's a place of cumulus cloudscapes, sudden downpours and steaming footpaths.

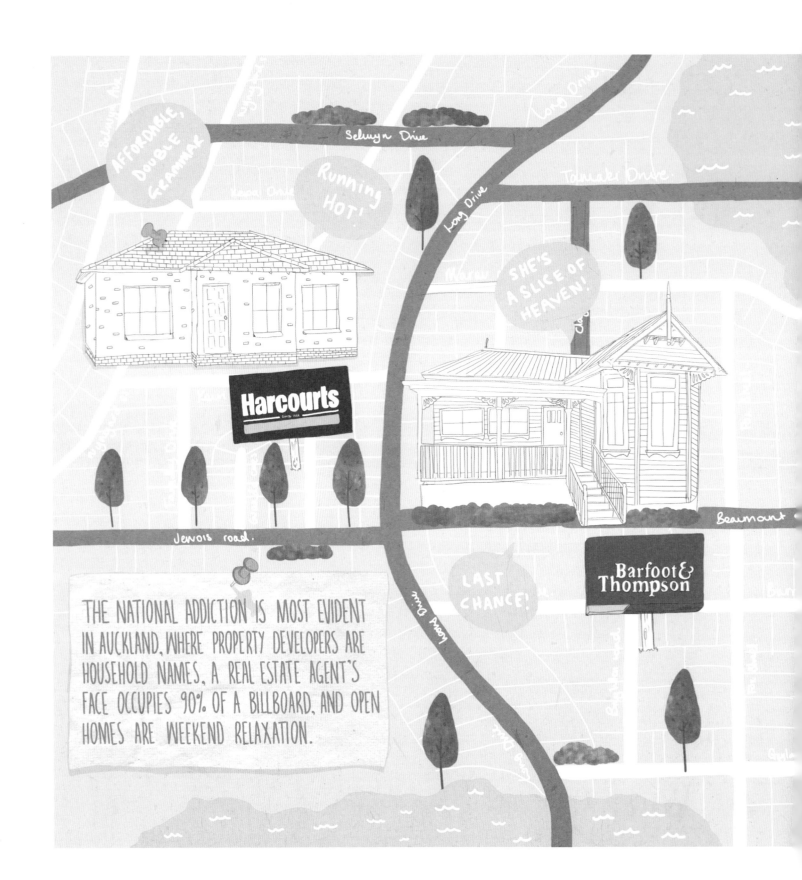

THE NATIONAL ADDICTION IS MOST EVIDENT IN AUCKLAND, WHERE PROPERTY DEVELOPERS ARE HOUSEHOLD NAMES, A REAL ESTATE AGENT'S FACE OCCUPIES 90% OF A BILLBOARD, AND OPEN HOMES ARE WEEKEND RELAXATION.

Auckland ~ Real ~ Estate

ASIDE FROM A SHORT BLIP DURING THE GFC IN 2008, AUCKLAND REAL ESTATE VALUES HAVE BEEN SOARING SINCE THE TURN OF THE MILLENNIUM. IN MID-2003 THE MEDIAN HOUSE PRICE REACHED A RECORD-HIGH $670,000, NEARLY A 20% RISE FROM A YEAR BEFORE. THIS SELLER'S MARKET HAS CREATED ITS OWN SPECTATOR SPORT IN THE FORM OF PACKED, HIGHLY-COMPETITIVE PROPERTY AUCTIONS.

Alice in Auck·er·land

ALICE IS THE GIANT AUCKLAND MOTORWAY TUNNELING MACHINE THAT IS UNDERTAKING A 2-YEAR UNDERGROUND JOURNEY FROM OWAIRAKA TO WATERVIEW AND BACK. THE RESULT OF THIS MULTI-BILLION DOLLAR PROJECT WILL BE 2.4KM TWIN TUNNELS WHICH WILL COMPLETE THE WESTERN RING ROUTE. ALICE TRAVELS AT UP TO 8CM A MINUTE, ABOUT AS FAST AS A SNAIL. 20,000 AUCKLANDERS SNAPPED UP TICKETS TO THE OPEN DAY. NAMED AFTER ALICE IN WONDERLAND, ALICE IS THE 10TH BIGGEST BORING MACHINE OF ITS KIND IN THE WORLD.

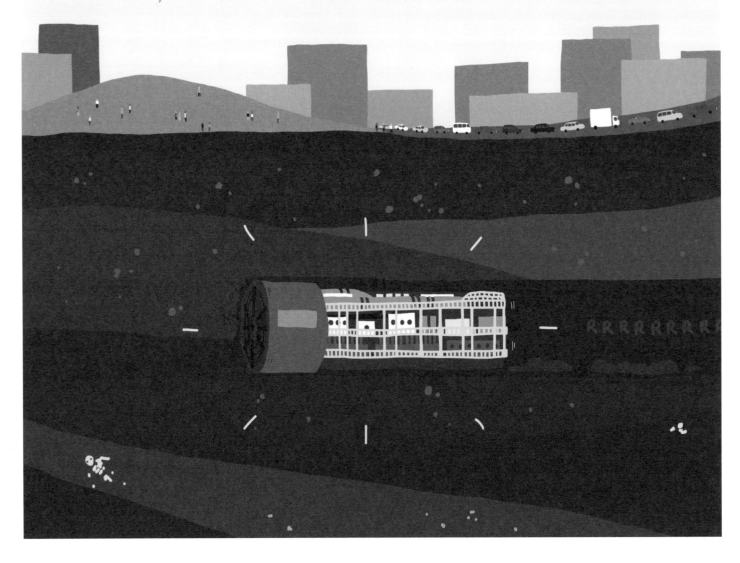

ALBERT PARK TUNNELS

With the introduction of Japan to WWII in 1941, Auckland suddenly felt nervous about its lack of air-raid shelters. In the event of a bombing, only a quarter of the population would fit under cover. So the idea was hatched to dig over 3.5 kms of tunnels beneath Albert Park that could hold 22,000 people. It took 114 council workers eight months to dig through the volcanic rock. Though the tunnels were never needed, a handful of Aucklanders still dream of getting citizens down into them for tourism, historical appreciation, or even to solve traffic problems.

Home of the Longkeeper

Auckland's original market gardeners were Māori, who were producing enough potatoes in the 1830s to export them to Sydney. Dalmation migrants in the 1890s covered Kumeu and the Oratia Valley with orchards and vineyards (Auckland's Fruit Bowl), and Indian and Chinese migrants kept Pukekohe soil at a premium throughout the 20th century (Auckland's Salad Bowl). Since the 80s the Pukekohe Longkeeper (an onion, NZ's highest-earning export vegetable), has been feeding Japan too. The volcanic loam of Auckland's foothills now produces one-third of NZ's fresh vegetables.

CHELSEA

SUGAR · REFINERY

SUGARLOAVES.

pink packaging

New Zealand's most densely-populated island, Waiheke, is home to viticulturalists, creatives, bistro-owners, eccentrics, the mega-rich, bio-warriors, and anyone else who wants to live on an island within shouting distance of Auckland. A quarter of its 8,000 residents commute to the city ~~each~~ daily. Over summer, however, the population can swell to 50,000, with the island hosting such cosmopolitan attractions as the Waiheke Island International Jazz Festival, the Waiheke Olive Festival, and the Waiheke Wine Festival, not to mention the Waiheke Walking Festival, in case the island's natural beauty was starting to get overlooked.

WAIHEKE

COME A HOT FRIDAY

AUCKLANDERS ARE EXPERTS AT MAKING THE MOST OF A LONG WEEKEND. UNDAUNTED BY ENDLESS TRAFFIC, THEY MIGRATE EN MASSE TO RUGGED NORTHERN BEACHES, THE IDYLLIC COROMANDEL AND TROUT-FILLED LAKES TO THE SOUTH.

THE NATURAL WORLD MIGHT BE
NEW ZEALAND'S CINEMATIC CANVAS,
BUT ON TV WE'RE AUCKLAND.
OUR NEWS IS READ HERE & OUR
MOST SUCCESSFUL TV DRAMAS SET
HERE —SUCH AS *NOTHING TRIVIAL*,
OUTRAGEOUS FORTUNE, *GLOSS* &
THE EVER-POPULAR *SHORTLAND
STREET* WHICH HAS NOW AIRED
MORE THAN 5,000 EPISODES.
PRIMETIME FAVOURITES, *THE BLOCK*,
MASTERCHEF & *NZ's GOT TALENT*
ARE ALL FILMED IN AUCKLAND.

LIGHTING UP THE NEW YEAR

AUCKLAND CELEBRATES THE CHINESE NEW YEAR WITH THE COLOURFUL, 4-DAY LANTERN FESTIVAL AT ALBERT PARK. THE POPULAR, NIGHT-TIME FESTIVAL SHOWCASES CHINESE ARTS AND CULTURE WITH OVER 800 LARGE, HAND-CRAFTED LANTERNS OF FIGURES AND ANIMALS, 500 PERFORMERS AND A FIREWORKS DISPLAY

JONES 1999

1996

OKISENE

JOHNSON 2011

WIKI 2005

GO THE WARRIORS!

THE WARRIORS HAVE BEEN WINNING THE HEARTS OF AUCKLANDERS SINCE THEY ENTERED THE AUSTRALIAN NRL COMPETITION IN 1995. THEY HAVE REACHED SEVEN PLAY-OFFS, TWO GRAND FINALS, WON ONE MINOR PREMIERSHIP. THEIR UNPREDICTABLE, ENTERTAINING STYLE OF PLAY HAS ENSURED UNBELIEVABLE WINS, BAFFLING LOSSES AND CREATED A FRESH GENERATION OF POLYNESIAN SPORT HEROES. WHERE THE WARRIORS HAVE DEFINITELY WON IS OFF THE FIELD - THEY ENJOY ONE OF SPORT'S MOST DEDICATED FAN BASES, INCLUDING, MOST FAMOUSLY, SIR PETER LEITCH, THE MAD BUTCHER.

VATUVEI

2008

MANNERING

2012

SIR PETER LEITCH

STANLEY STREET

Stanley Street has hosted local tennis matches since 1920 and an international tournament since 1956. Today the womens ASB Classic and mens Heineken Open are held in the two weeks before the Australian Open, attracting many high-ranking players. Major renovations have added to the glamour of the venue - a rooftop swimming pool, beauty salon, spas and saunas, sliding roof, and New Zealand's most comprehensive gym.

Night Markets

Wherever you are in Auckland, you're never far away from a night market. After dark, Aucklanders flock to markets in Onehunga, Papatoetoe, Glenfield, Whangaparaoa, Pakuranga and Silo Park to enjoy delicious foods, fresh produce, arts and crafts, and no shortage of live entertainment.

manukau

Manukau is the most ethnically diverse urban area in the country. Its 335,000 people now include 160 different ethnic groups, the largest Polynesian population in the world and the largest Māori population in New Zealand. Samoan is the second most spoken language in Manukau, after English. Manukau's population is young (40% under 24) and growing (around 10,000 extra people a year). The wading birds of the nearby Manukau Harbour (NZ's second largest) gave the area its name.

THE NINES

Aucklanders' love of rugby league reaches fever pitch at the NRL Nines, a two-day, nine-a-side tournament that sees crowds of 45,000, many in fancy dress, roaring on their favourites.

COOK ISLANDS

HAWAII

AOTEAROA

TONGA

KIRIBATI

NIUE

POLYFEST

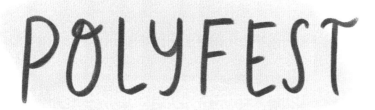

AUCKLAND CITY HAS DECLARED MARCH 'PACIFIC AS':
A FANTASTIC CELEBRATION OF PACIFIC CULTURE.
IN POLYFEST, AT THE MANUKAU SPORTS BOWL, 9,000
STUDENTS SING & SALSA IN FRONT OF 10,000 PEOPLE.
POLYFEST'S BIG SISTER, PASIFIKA, IS HELD AT WESTERN
SPRINGS AND IS THE LARGEST PASIFIC FESTIVAL IN THE
WORLD. IT SHOWCASES 11 ISLAND COMMUNITIES
THROUGH THEIR ARTS, PERFORMANCES AND THEIR
TRADITIONAL FOOD.

SAMOA

FIJI

TOKELAU

TUVALU

TAHITI

THE GATEWAY

Auckland's airport is NZ's international gateway, handling nearly 15 million passengers a year—around half of them international travellers. At its busiest, the airport handles over 40 take-offs and landings an hour. Planes have been using the Mangere site since 1928, although it wasn't developed into the city's main airport until 1966. The main road to the airport is named after pioneer aviator George Bolt, who delivered NZ's first airmail in 1919.

OTARA MARKET

STARTED IN THE EARLY 80S, OTARA MARKET IS THE WORLD'S LARGEST POLYNESIAN MARKET. EVERY SATURDAY MORNING, THE MARKET TEEMS WITH SHOPPERS BUYING EVERYTHING FROM BARGAIN-PRICED FRESH FRUIT AND VEGIES TO CRAFTS, CLOTHING AND ISLAND MUSIC CDS. A GREAT ARRAY OF EXOTIC FOODS ARE ON OFFER — PACIFIC, ASIAN, AND OTHER CULTURES. CULTURAL PERFORMANCES AND LIVELY MUSIC ADD TO THE VIBRANT ATMOSPHERE. THESE DAYS MANY STALLS ARE RUN BY ASIAN PEOPLE AS WELL AS PACIFIC.

LIME $24⁹⁹ KG

CARROTS .99¢ KG

LEEKS $2⁴⁹

MEGA-MALLS

DRESS SMART

LYNNMALL

WESTFIELD MALLS

277 NEWMARKET

SYLVIA PARK

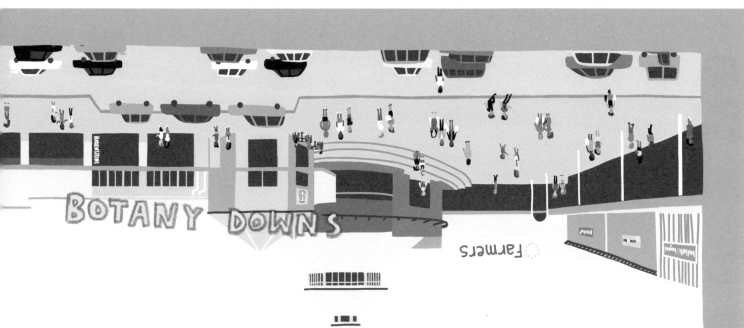

AUCKLAND'S LOVE AFFAIR WITH MALLS BEGAN IN 1963 WITH THE CONSTRUCTION OF THE FIRST MALL IN NEW LYNN, AND HAS BEEN GOING STRONG EVER SINCE. STAND-OUTS INCLUDE MEGA MALLS SYLVIA PARK WITH MORE THAN 200 STORES AND BOTANY DOWNS WITH 150 STORES. THESE SELF-CONTAINED VILLAGES OFFER HUGE CHOICE, CLIMATE CONTROLLED ENVIRONMENTS AND CAR PARKS BY THE HECTARE. THE THOUSANDS OF SQUARE METRES OF RETAIL SPACE MAKE SHOPPING A LEGITIMATE FORM OF EXERCISE, SO MUCH SO THAT SOME MALLS ISSUE SHOPPERS WITH PEDOMETERS.

the KARAKA
horse sales

THE ANNUAL YEARLING SALES AT KARAKA, IN SOUTH AUCKLAND, ARE A SHOWCASE FOR NZ'S RACING INDUSTRY AND TOP-PERFORMING RACEHORSES. THE EVENT, AUSTRALASIA'S LEADING AUCTION FOR TWO-YEAR-OLD THOROUGHBREDS, ATTRACTS BIDDERS FROM AROUND THE WORLD AND TURNS OVER $50 MILLION.

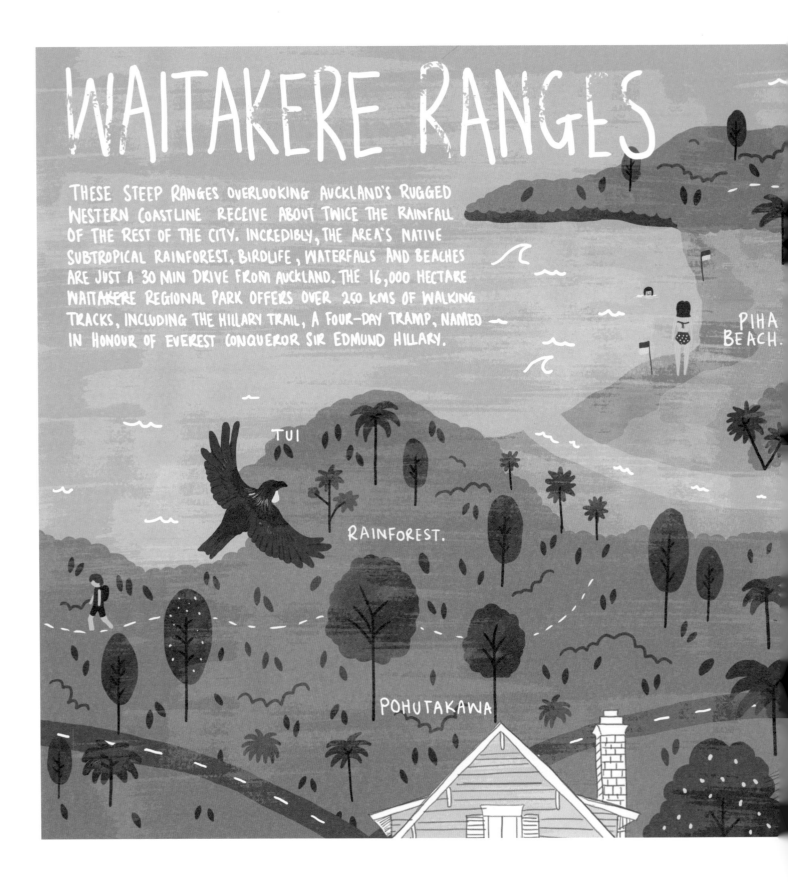

WAITAKERE RANGES

THESE STEEP RANGES OVERLOOKING AUCKLAND'S RUGGED WESTERN COASTLINE RECEIVE ABOUT TWICE THE RAINFALL OF THE REST OF THE CITY. INCREDIBLY, THE AREA'S NATIVE SUBTROPICAL RAINFOREST, BIRDLIFE, WATERFALLS AND BEACHES ARE JUST A 30 MIN DRIVE FROM AUCKLAND. THE 16,000 HECTARE WAITAKERE REGIONAL PARK OFFERS OVER 250 KMS OF WALKING TRACKS, INCLUDING THE HILLARY TRAIL, A FOUR-DAY TRAMP, NAMED IN HONOUR OF EVEREST CONQUEROR SIR EDMUND HILLARY.

PIHA BEACH.

TUI

RAINFOREST.

POHUTAKAWA

the Black Sands
out West

Auckland's spectacular black sand west coast beaches — Karekare, Muriwai, Piha, Te Henga, Whatipu, Ananhata etc. — are just 40 minutes drive from the city. Their black sand is evidence of volcanic origins. Piha is home to Lion Rock, a 16-million-year-old volcanic neck that once held a Māori pa. The water along this rugged coastline is notoriously dangerous, but irresistable to fishers, surfers and swimmers. A popular TV series, *Piha Rescue*, showcases the heroics of local lifesavers.

The Barrier is the fourth largest island in New Zealand's main chain. Captain Cook named it after the Barrier formed between the Hauraki Gulf and the open sea. Home to 852 people, half of its households have only one person. In 1896 its isolation gave rise to a pigeon-gram service to Auckland, using the world's first airmail stamps. Today 40% of households have internet, but with no street lighting, no electricity grid, and no secondary schools, it remains the New Zealand of a lost era. In summer, visitors push the island's population to 3,000.

GREAT
BARRIER
ISLAND

THE WRITERS

MICHAEL FITZSIMONS

CONCEPTS, ART DIRECTION,
TEXT, WINE-TASTING,
FURNITURE REMOVALS

NIGEL BECKFORD

CONCEPTS, ART DIRECTION,
TEXT, SINGING, DOG-WALKING

PATRICK FITZSIMONS

RESEARCH, TEXT

THE ILLUSTRATORS

EZRA WHITTAKER-POWLEY

SARAH RYAN

CYNTHIA MERHEJ

ALISHA BRUNTON

IVY NIU

SANDI MACKECHNIE

JESS LUNNON

THE ILLUSTRATIONS

EZRA WHITTAKER-POWLEY

PAGES 36/37, 38/39, 60/61, 62/63, 68/69, 76/77, 90/91, 94, 95, 116/117, 120/121, 126/127

SARAH RYAN

PAGES 9, 10, 22/23, 30/31, 44/45, 47, 74/75, 92/93, 96, 97, 124/125

CYNTHIA MERHEJ

PAGES 20/21, 66/67, 70/71, 82/83, 84, 85, 86/87

ALISHA BRUNTON

PAGES 56/57, 58/59, 72/73, 78/79, 88/89, 106, 107, 108/109, 110/111, 112/113, 118/119, 122/123

IVY NIU

PAGES 24/25, 26/27, 28/29, 32/33, 34/35, 46, 48, 49, 50/51, 52/53, 54, 80/81, 104/105, 114/115

JESS LUNNON AND SANDI MACKECHNIE

PAGES 4/5, 6/7, 8, 11, 12/13, 14/15, 16/17, 18/19, 40/41, 42/43, 55, 64/65, 98/99, 100/101, 102/103, 128

Meet the Publishers

Nigel Beckford and Michael Fitzsimons are professional writers and run a communications and publishing firm, FitzBeck Creative. They've collaborated on numerous books and writing projects, including *With a Passion, The Extraordinary Passions of Ordinary New Zealanders, You Don't take a Big Leap Without a Gulp: Finding the Courage to Change Careers and Live Again, Navigators: Pacific Health Leaders Tell their Stories* and *Te Paruhi a Nga Takuta, Interviews with Māori Medical Practitioners*. They collaborated with a team of illustrators to produce *The Wellington Book* and *The NZ Book*. These books earned them Best Awards in 2011 and 2012 in the editorial and books section for their writing and art direction.